Ben Parker

EASY
RECORDER
TUNES

30 Fun and Easy Recorder Tunes for Beginners

Author: Ben Parker

Editor: Alison McNicol

First published in 2014 by Kyle Craig Publishing

This version updated Dec 2014

Text and illustration copyright © 2014 Kyle Craig Publishing

Design and illustration: Julie Anson

Music set by Ben Parker using Sibelius software

ISBN: 978-1-908707-36-9

A CIP record for this book is available from the British Library.

A Kyle Craig Publication

www.kyle-craig.com

Contents

WELCOME!

Welcome to '**30 Easy Recorder Tunes**'. Before you are ready to use this book you should have either already used my great '**My First Recorder**' book, or learned the basic recorder notes listed below. This book is full of fun and easy tunes that will help you practice and progress your recorder playing skills, plus you will learn a few new notes to help take your playing to the next level! Below is a reminder of the basic notes you will have learned so far, and we will show you any new notes to learn at the start of each tune. Happy playing!

Your Notes So Far

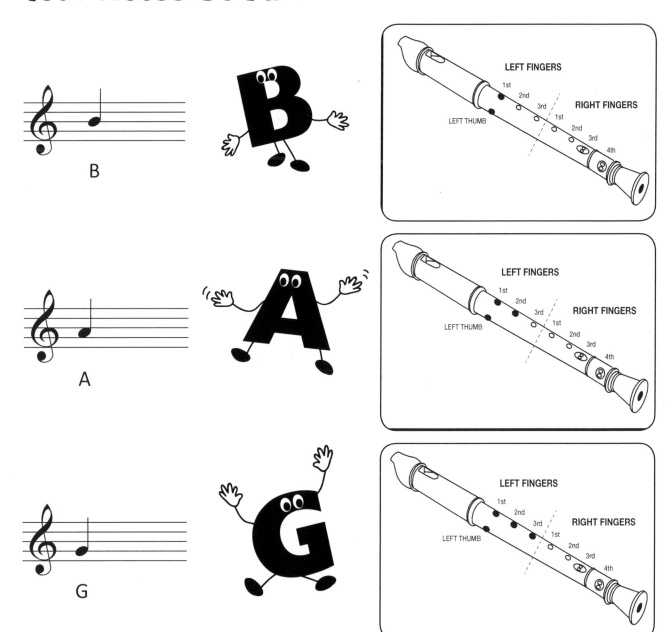

B

A

G

E

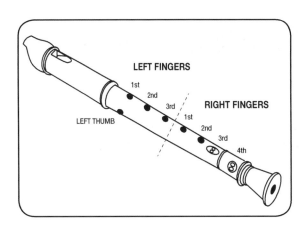

LEFT FINGERS

LEFT THUMB

1st
2nd
3rd

RIGHT FINGERS

1st
2nd
3rd
4th

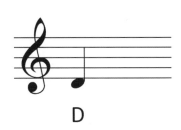

D

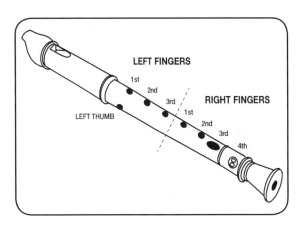

LEFT FINGERS

LEFT THUMB

1st
2nd
3rd

RIGHT FINGERS

1st
2nd
3rd
4th

C'

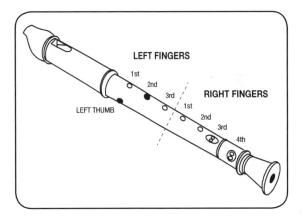

LEFT FINGERS

LEFT THUMB

1st
2nd
3rd

RIGHT FINGERS

1st
2nd
3rd
4th

D'

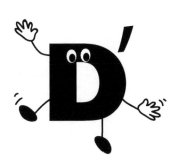

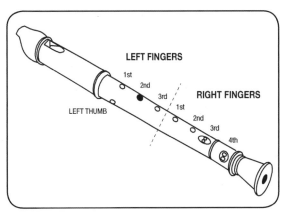

LEFT FINGERS

LEFT THUMB

1st
2nd
3rd

RIGHT FINGERS

1st
2nd
3rd
4th

Au Clare De La Lune

Ode To Joy

Drink To Me Only

Drink to me on - ly with thine eyes and I will pledge with mine.

Oh When The Saints

Oh when the saints, oh when the saints, oh when the saints go march - ing in. I want to be in that num - ber when the saints go march - ing in.

Jingle Bells

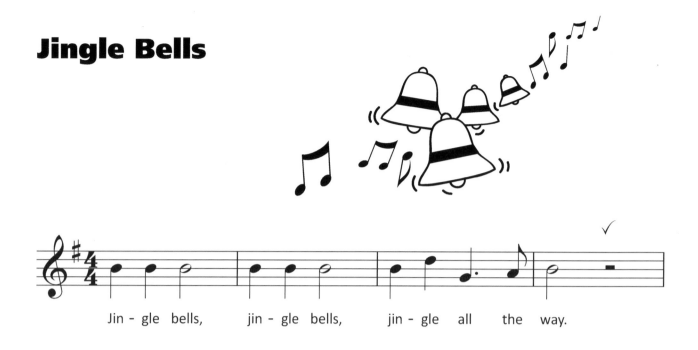

Jin - gle bells, jin - gle bells, jin - gle all the way.

Oh what fun it is to ride in a one horse o - pen sleigh, hey!

Jin - gle bells, jin - gle bells, jin - gle all the way

Oh what fun it is to ride in a one horse o - pen sleigh,

Oranges And Lemons

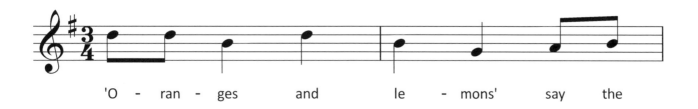

'O - ran - ges and le - mons' say the

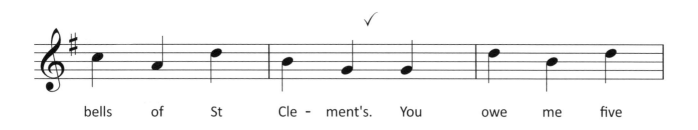

bells of St Cle - ment's. You owe me five

far - things' say the bells of St Mar - tin's.

Old MacDonald

Old Mac - Don - ald had a farm ee - i - ee - i oh. And

on that farm he had some chi ckens ee - i - ee - i oh. With a

cluck cluck here and a cluck cluck there, here a cluck, there a cluck,

ev - ery - where a cluck cluck. Old Mac - Don - ald

had a farm ee - i - ee - i oh.

Hush Little Baby

Hush lit-tle ba-by don't say a word, ma-ma's gon na buy you a

mock-ing bird. And if that mock-ing bird don't sing,

ma-ma's gon-na buy you a dia-mond ring.

Dear Liza

There's a hole in my buck-et dear Li-za, dear Li-za. There's a

hole in my buck-et dear Li-za a hole.

Amazing Grace

A - maz - ing___ grace, how sweet the sound that

saved a___ wretch like___ me._____ I___

once was___ lost, but now am found; was___

blind but___ now I see._____

Good King Wenceslas

*NEW NOTE REMINDER

Good King Wen - ces - las looked out on the feast of Ste - phen,

when the snow lay round a - bout, deep and crisp and e - ven.

Bright - ly shone the moon that night, though the frost was cru - el.

when a poor man came in sight, gath - ering win - ter fu - el.

A useful note reminder will be shown when new notes are introduced

Grand Old Duke Of York

Oh the grand old Duke of York, he had ten thou-sand men, he marched them up to the top of the hill and he marched them down a - gain.

Skip To My Lou

Skip, skip, skip to my Lou. Skip, skip, skip to my Lou. Skip, skip, skip to my Lou. Skip to my Lou, my dar - ling.

This Old Man

This old man, he played one, he played knick- knack

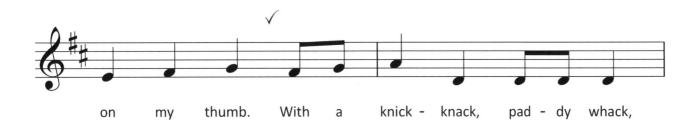

on my thumb. With a knick - knack, pad - dy whack,

give the dog a bone. This old man came roll - ing home.

I Saw Three Ships

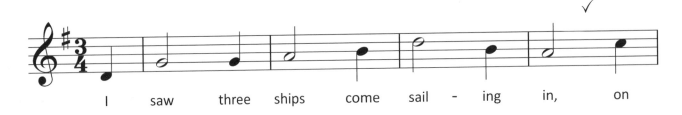

I saw three ships come sail - ing in, on

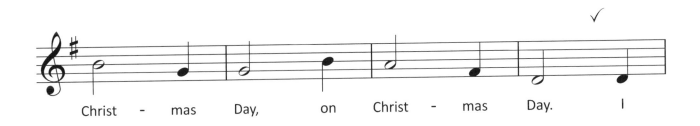

Christ - mas Day, on Christ - mas Day. I

saw three ships come sail - ing in, on

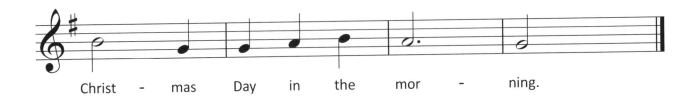

Christ - mas Day in the mor - ning.

Song Of The Volga Boatmen

Yo, yo, heave ho! Oh, yo, yo, heave ho!

Pull to - ge - ther; for - ward we go.

Humpty Dumpty

Hump - ty Dump - ty sat on a wall.

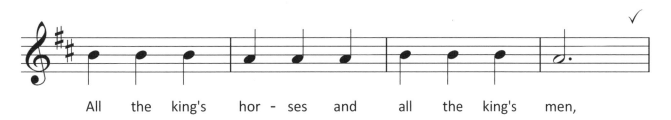

Hump - ty Dump - ty had a great fall.

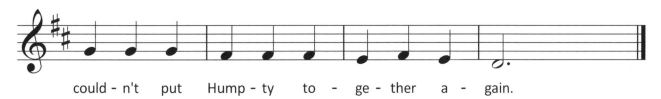

All the king's hor - ses and all the king's men,

could - n't put Hump - ty to - ge - ther a - gain.

Clementine

Oh my dar - ling, oh my dar - ling, oh my

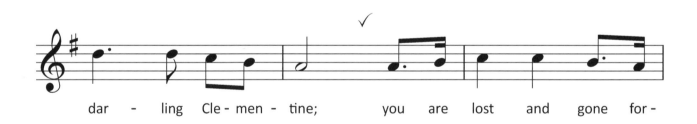

dar - ling Cle - men - tine; you are lost and gone for -

ev - er dread - ful sor - ry Cle - men - tine.

We Three Kings Of Orient Are

We three kings of O - ri - ent are, bear - ing gifts we

tra - vel so far. Field and foun - tain, moor and mount - ain

fol - low - ing yon - der star. Oh_____ star of won - der,

star of night, star with roy - al beau - ty bright. West - ward lead - ing,

still pro - ceed - ing, guide us to thy per - fect light.

Home On The Range

Oh, give me a home where the buf - fa - lo roam, where the

deer and the an - te - lope play,_____ where

sel - dom is heard a dis - cou - ra - ging word and the

skies are not cloud - y all day._____

Kumbaya

Kum - ba - ya my Lord,_____ Kum - ba - ya._____ Kum - ba -

ya my Lord,_____ Kum - ba - ya._____ Kum - ba -

ya my Lord,_____ Kum - ba - ya._____

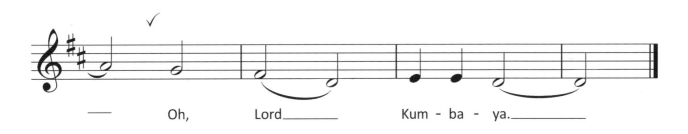

— Oh, Lord_____ Kum - ba - ya._____

Streets Of Laredo

As I was out walk - ing the streets of La - re - do, as

I walked out in La - re - do one day, I

met a young cow - boy all dressed in white li - nen, all

dressed in white li - nen and cold as the day.

Oh Little Town Of Bethlehem

top E

LEFT FINGERS
1st
2nd
3rd
LEFT THUMB
Covers **HALF** the hole
RIGHT FINGERS
1st
2nd
3rd
4th

Oh   lit - tle town of   Beth - le - hem how   still   we__ see thee

lie.   A - bove thy deep and   dream - less__ sleep the

si - lent__ stars go   by.   Yet__   in   thy dark__ streets

shi - neth the   ev - er   last - ing   light,   the

hopes and fears of   all__ the__ years are   met in__ thee to - night.

My Bonnie

My Bon - nie lies o - ver the o - cean._____ My
Bon - nie lies o - ver the sea._____ My
Bon - nie lies o - ver the o - cean,_____ oh
bring back my Bon - nie to me._____

Swing Low, Sweet Chariot

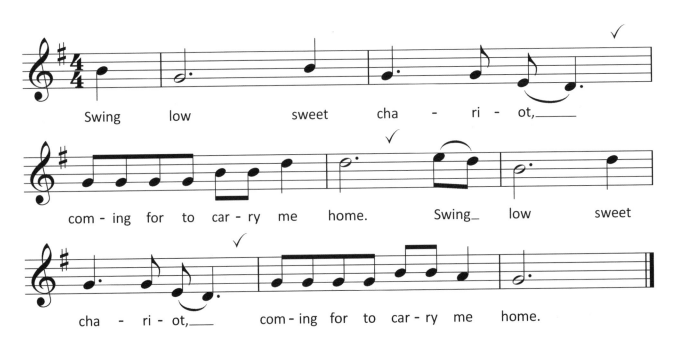

Swing low sweet cha - ri - ot,_____
com - ing for to car - ry me home. Swing_ low sweet
cha - ri - ot,____ com - ing for to car - ry me home.

We Wish You A Merry Christmas

bottom C

LEFT FINGERS
RIGHT FINGERS
LEFT THUMB
1st 2nd 3rd 1st 2nd 3rd 4th

We wish you a mer-ry Christ-mas, we wish you a mer-ry

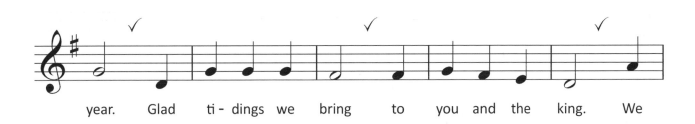

Christ-mas, we wish you a mer-ry Christ-mas and a hap-py new

Glad ti-dings we bring to you and the king. We

wish you a mer-ry Christ-mas and a hap-py new year.

year.

Silent Night

top F natural

Si - lent night, ho - ly night.

All is calm, all is bright.

Round yon vir - gin__ mo - ther and child,

ho - ly in - fant so ten - der and

mild. Sleep in hea - ven - ly peace,_____

sleep__ in hea - ven - ly peace._____

Comin' Round The Mountain

top **G**

She'll be com - in' round the moun-tain when she comes. She'll be

com - in' round the moun-tain when she comes. She'll be

com - in' round the moun-tain, com - in' round the moun-tain,

com - in' round the moun-tain when she comes.

Scotland The Brave

C

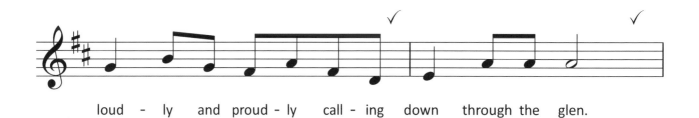

Hark, when the night is fall - ing, hear, hear the pipes are call - ing

loud - ly and proud - ly call - ing down through the glen.

There, where the hills are sleep - ing now feel the blood a - leap - ing

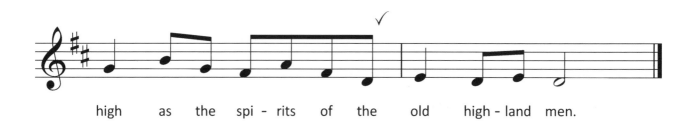

high as the spi - rits of the old high - land men.

Andulko The Goose Girl

An - dul - ko, are you at home my dear? There's

no time to wait. All your fat geese have es -

caped I fear: they ran through the gate.

All your geese in the corn. Call them

in, here it's morn. An - dul - ko quick - ly come

down, my dear, be - fore it's too late.

MORE GREAT MUSIC BOOKS FROM KYLE CRAIG!

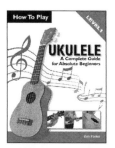

How To Play UKULELE — A Complete Guide for Absolute Beginners

978-1-908-707-08-6

My First UKULELE — Learn to Play: Kids

978-1-908-707-11-6

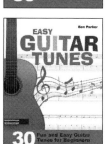

Easy UKULELE Tunes

978-1-908707-37-6

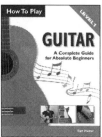

How To Play GUITAR — A Complete Guide for Absolute Beginners

978-1-908-707-09-3

My First GUITAR — Learn to Play: Kids

978-1-908-707-13-0

Easy GUITAR Tunes

978-1-908707-34-5

How To Play KEYBOARD — A Complete Guide for Absolute Beginners

978-1-908-707-14-7

My First KEYBOARD — Learn to Play: Kids

978-1-908-707-15-4

Easy KEYBOARD Tunes

978-1-908707-35-2

How To Play PIANO — A Complete Guide for Absolute Beginners

978-1-908-707-16-1

My First PIANO — Learn to Play: Kids

978-1-908-707-17-8

Easy PIANO Tunes

978-1-908707-33-8

How To Play HARMONICA — A Complete Guide for Absolute Beginners

978-1-908-707-28-4

My First RECORDER — Learn to Play: Kids

978-1-908-707-18-5

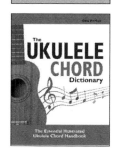

Easy RECORDER Tunes

978-1-908707-36-9

How To Play BANJO — A Complete Guide for Absolute Beginners

978-1-908-707-19-2

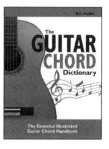

The GUITAR Chord Dictionary

978-1-908707-39-0

The UKULELE Chord Dictionary

978-1-908707-38-3

Made in the USA
Columbia, SC
21 November 2021

49430814R00017